P9-DZX-740

SING AND READ STORYBOOK™

Jingle Bells

SCHOLASTIC INC.
Cartwheel B·O·O·K·S®

New York   Toronto   London   Auckland   Sydney
Mexico City   New Delhi   Hong Kong   Buenos Aires

To our good friends and neighbors
in the beautiful Schoharie Valley

No part of this publication may be reproduced, or stored in a retrieval system, or transmitted in any form or by any means, electronic, mechanical, photocopying, recording, or otherwise, without written permission of the publisher. For information regarding permission, write to Scholastic Inc., Attention: Permissions Department, 555 Broadway, New York, NY 10012.

ISBN 0-439-28721-9

Copyright © 2001 by Scholastic Inc. Illustrations copyright © 2001 by Darcy May.
All rights reserved. Published by Scholastic Inc.
SCHOLASTIC, CARTWHEEL BOOKS, SING AND READ STORY BOOK, and associated logos are trademarks and/or registered trademarks of Scholastic Inc.

20 19 18 17 16 15   10 11 12/0

Printed in the U.S.A.   40
First printing, November 2001

Dashing through the snow

In a one-horse open sleigh,

Through the fields we go

Laughing all the way,

Bells on bobtail ring,

Making spirits bright;

What fun it is to ride and sing
a sleighing song tonight!

Jingle bells! Jingle bells!

Jingle all the way!

Oh, what fun it is to ride

In a one-horse open sleigh.

Ooh!
Jingle bells! Jingle bells!

Jingle all the way!

Oh, what fun it is to ride

In a one-horse open sleigh!

Jingle Bells